FOOTSTEPS TO GLORY

12 Drama Sketches for Lent and Holy Week

PETER JACKSON

kevin mayhew

First published in 2007 by
KEVIN MAYHEW LTD
Buxhall, Stowmarket, Suffolk IP14 3BW
info@kevinmayhewltd.com
www.kevinmayhew.com

© 2007 Peter Jackson

The right of Peter Jackson to be identified as the author of this work has been asserted by him in accordance with the Copyright, Designs and Patents Act 1988. All rights reserved.

Scripture quotations are taken from the New International Version, copyright © 1973, 1978, 1984 International Bible Society. Used by permission of Zondervan Bible Publishers.

The sketches in this book may be photocopied without copyright infringement, provided they are used for the purpose for which they are intended. Reproduction of any of the contents of this book for commercial purposes is subject to the usual copyright restrictions.

All rights reserved.

9 8 7 6 5 4 3 2 1 0

ISBN 978 1 84417 841 4
Catalogue No. 1501048

Cover design by Sara-Jane Came
Typsetting by Richard Weaver

Printed and bound in Great Britain

Contents

About the Author

Peter Jackson is a writer and editor living in Crowborough, East Sussex. From 1998-99 he edited the monthly magazine *Celebrate* for The Church of England and is a lay preacher at his parish church. Interested in drama from an early age (a non-speaking galleon in Sheridan's *The Critic*) until the present (God in *The Mysteries)* he was assistant editor of the theatre magazine *Plays and Players* early in his journalistic career. A published author of business communication books he has also written plays and sketches for school and church groups, particularly The Rainbow Drama Group of All Saints, Crowborough.

Ten of his Christian sketches for children – including three nativity plays – have been published by Kevin Mayhew as *The Star and the Stable* as well as a wide variety of sketches for church drama groups in *Acts of Faith, 25 Christian Drama Sketches* and, most recently, *The Coming King* – sketches for Advent and Christmas.

Introduction

Easter is the perfect time to bring drama into your church service or group meeting. In the Middle Ages it was the Christian Church that revived a struggling art form by dramatising parts of the Latin service so that the congregation could more easily understand Christianity, particularly the Easter story.

Today, many at church on Good Friday and Easter Sunday may be nominal churchgoers or visiting relatives or friends pressed into service. A well-acted and well-produced piece of drama to add point to the reading and talk or sermon may be just what is required to give a better understanding of the events of Lent and Holy Week – in themselves the greatest piece of drama the world has ever seen.

These twelve sketches are shaped in two distinct blocks. The five for the Sundays in Lent are each based on one of the set Bible passages for that day but, rather than repeat the action of the reading, aim to put the key message into a relevant application for today's Christians.

The seven short dramas for Palm Sunday to Easter Day again take one of the set readings to provide the Bible-based context but go on to develop it as an exchange between two characters in the story; sometimes at the centre but mostly on the fringe. In every case the Bible reading forms part of the sketch.

In each sketch **performance time** will give you a rough idea whether the script will fit the slot available. The **wording** of the scripts, although carefully considered for performance, is not sacrosanct and you are, of course, free to change names, places, characters and swap male and female members of the cast if it makes the sketch more appropriate to your needs and resources. **Stage directions** are always from the actors' viewpoint.

Let me acknowledge a debt of **inspiration** for the content of some sketches to Clive Sansom's biblical poetry collection *The Witnesses* (now, regrettably, out of print), Joyce Huggett's readings and prayers for Lent *God's Springtime* (Kevin Mayhew) and the various authors of the Matthew, Luke and John volumes of *The NIV Application Commentary* (Zondervan).

You will use these sketches as you see fit; as stand-alone supports to a single talk or sermon, as part of a Lent series covering several weeks or perhaps in a block of six or seven, interleaved with songs and hymns as a Good Friday presentation. However you use them, join your prayer with mine that at each performance they will lead someone, somewhere, to follow in Jesus of Nazareth's footsteps to glory.

First Sunday in Lent

Resistance

Lent begins with the story of Jesus' forty days of testing in the dry heat of the desert; such a contrast with Adam's time of trial in the lush greenery of Eden. But where Adam succumbed to temptation, this second Adam triumphed, blunting the spurious offers of wealth, power and independence from God with cast-iron nuggets of Scripture. This sketch underlines the worldly plausibility by which similar testing may come to us today.

Bible source Luke 4:1-13

Performance time Ten minutes with reading

Characters Reader
Sir Alex Stonor – a self-made businessman (and proud of it)
Felicity Weston – his PA
Michael Standish – a graduate trainee

Scene setter *The CEO's office at Mammon Holdings Plc – as grand as time and space will allow. A table/desk with phone, papers etc. Strategically placed potted palms and uplighters will help to create the atmosphere as will a large executive chair for Stonor who is sitting in it reading* The Financial Times. *The company name should be visible in some way. Felicity and Standish are off Left. If possible the office scene should be in darkness while the Reader, spotlit, is on stage. Even with a daytime production some contrast can be achieved by the use of uplighters and lamps.*

The Reader enters and takes centre stage.

Reader Jesus is tempted in the desert.

Jesus, full of the Holy Spirit, returned from the Jordan and was led by the Spirit in the desert, where for forty days he was tempted by the devil. He ate nothing during those days, and at the end of them he was hungry.

The devil said to him, 'If you are the Son of God, tell this stone to become bread.'

Jesus answered, 'It is written: "Man does not live on bread alone."'

The devil led him up to a high place and showed him in an instant all the kingdoms of the world. And he said to him, 'I will give you all their authority and splendour, for it has been given to me, and I can give it to anyone I want to. So if you worship me, it will all be yours.'

Jesus answered, 'It is written: "Worship the Lord your God and serve him only."'

The devil led him to Jerusalem and had him stand on the highest point of the temple. 'If you are the Son of God,' he said, 'throw yourself down from here. For it is written: "He will command his angels concerning you to guard you carefully; they will lift you up in their hands, so that you will not strike your foot against a stone."'

Jesus answered, 'It says: "Do not put the Lord your God to the test."'

When the devil had finished all this tempting, he left him until an opportune time.

The Reader exits. The office scene lights up. Stonor puts down his paper, checks his watch and presses an intercom button.

Stonor I'll see Standish now, Felicity.

He gets up, strolls to the back of the acting area and gazes out of the imaginary window, back to the audience.

Felicity *(Entering Left)* Mr Standish. *(She ushers Standish in and speaks to Stonor)* Coffee, Sir Alex?

Stonor Please. Oh, and tell Farmer I'll need him for the project meeting at – er *(glances at watch)* twelve forty-five.

Felicity Very good, Sir Alex. *(She exits)*

Stonor *(Comes round the desk and shakes Standish by the hand)* Good to meet you Standish. Michael, isn't it?

Standish Yes, Sir Alex. And we *have* met before. At the graduate intake reception.

Stonor Oh, yes. But I don't call that *meeting* someone. Second-rate wine and sausages on sticks and polite conversation. That's just to 'maintain good employee relations' as the HR crowd say. No, what I call meeting someone is the opportunity to find out what makes them tick, what they can do for Mammon Holdings and *(he pats Standish on the shoulder)* what Mammon Holdings can do for them.

Standish Well as to that, Sir Alex, I ought to tell you . . .

Stonor *(Moving back round the desk and eventually sitting down)* Take a seat, Michael. *(Waves hand)* Take a seat.

Knock off-Left. Felicity enters with tray, cups, cafetière, etc.

Felicity Your coffee, Sir Alex. *(Puts them on the desk)* Will that be all?

Stonor Nothing more for now. Did you tell Farmer?

Felicity Yes, he'll be here in twenty minutes. *(Moves to the door Left and exits, speaking to Standish as she passes)* Good luck Michael.

Standish Oh, thanks.

Stonor You know each other?

Standish Yes. Flic – er Miss Weston and I were at school together. *(He grins)* A long time ago!

Stonor *(Slightly irritated by this information)* Yes, well time goes on, Michael. Time goes on. And time, as they tell you in these management training books *(he gestures to imaginary bookshelves right)* which I've never read, means money. *(During next dialogue he stands to pour coffee for them both)* Now, let me get to the point. I've had good reports of your work from Hemsley and I have something in mind which I think will suit both of us very well.

Standish That sounds very encouraging but I should tell you that . . .

Stonor *(Waving him quiet)* All in good time, Michael. You don't know what I'm going to say yet! Now, you've heard about Project Asia?

Standish Oh yes. Mammon Holdings counter-attack on the Asian commercial giants. Using cheap labour in Eastern Europe to mass-produce consumer goods specifically designed for the Asian market. Beating them at their own game, so to speak. It's certainly a novel idea.

Stonor Novel? It's brilliant, Michael. It's what I learned all those years ago as an East End market trader. If someone's offering the punters a better deal than you, find a way of undercutting him, whatever it takes. Yes, Project Asia will take us to new heights of trading and profit Michael, and that's where you come in.

Standish Me, Sir Alex?

Stonor Yes. We're opening a new office in Hong Kong next month and I want you to be there as part of the team. There's a lot of young executives in the big Chinese and Japanese companies these days. I want you to mix with them, socialise with them, get them round to our way of thinking. I know you can do it; I've been watching your progress. *(Checks watch)* Farmer will be here shortly. He's leading the team and you can work out the details with him.

Standish Hong Kong? Well, it's a great offer Sir Alex but . . .

Stonor No need to thank me, Michael. Just do the job. That's all the thanks I want. Now, where's that agenda?

He turns to sort out a file of papers.

Standish I'm afraid that won't be possible, Sir Alex.

Stonor *(Stopped in mid flow)* What? What won't be possible?

Standish Doing the job. Going to Hong Kong. I've been trying to tell you since I came in. I'm not taking up the employment option.

Stonor *(Put out by this)* Not taking up the employment option? Who's put that idea into your head?

Standish Actually it was one of the induction course films – on the African company. Behind the plate glass of the offices and the production figures of the mines and the factories were these faces, faces of ordinary Africans who had no chance of improving themselves, no chance of moving on in the world, moving up to a better life. So I'm signing up on a teaching contract at a township school.

Stonor *(Annoyed but calm)* I see. Well, that's all very commendable, Michael. I have to admire your spirit – but I think it's misplaced. *(Pause)* How much are you getting for this – teaching Africans?

Standish Oh, bed and board in the hostel and around fifteen thousand.

Stonor Around fifteen thousand. That's a joke, isn't it? In Hong Kong you'd be earning fifty in the first year plus bonuses. And then there's a share option. *(Leans forward, fatherlike, and touches Standish's arm)* Michael, this is a material world. You need money to make your way in it, to buy the things you need. There's nothing wrong in that; there's no disgrace in working hard and earning a good salary. Think what you could do with fifty thousand. What you could buy for those African children of yours.

Standish But that's too easy, isn't it. That's just buying my way out of my responsibility. *(To himself)* The Spirit of the Lord is on me, because he has anointed me to preach good news to the poor.

Stonor *(Gets up and walks over stage Left to imaginary wall map)* You see this map, young man. Could be the old British Empire couldn't it, all those countries coloured red. But it's not. It's the operational spread of Mammon Holdings. Europe, Asia, the Middle East, North and South America, the Pacific Rim. *(Turns towards Standish)* The world is our oyster, young man and you can be part of it. You'll have power, influence. You can do more for the Third World working for me than in some tinpot school in Timbuktu.

Standish Perhaps I could, perhaps not. *(To himself)* What good is it for a man to gain the whole world, yet forfeit his soul?

Stonor *(Gets up and moves to window at back)* Come over here. *(Standish gets up and joins Stonor at the window, both with backs to audience)* Look out there, Standish. It's a brutal world, a dangerous world. I've known that, seen what it can do to a man. That's why I've built up Mammon Holdings. To protect me, wrap me in comfort, give me power, stop Alex Stonor falling down into the miserable existence of the millions out there who live and die without experiencing the real meaning of life. You can have that power, Standish. Just say 'yes' to Hong Kong.

Standish *(Walking back to his seat and standing beside it)* The real meaning of life, Sir Alex. What is that exactly? *(To himself)* To act justly and to love mercy and to walk humbly with your God.

Stonor *(Turns back from the window)* So what's it to be, Standish? Farmer will be here soon. Shall I tell him you'll be part of the team?

Standish I'm truly grateful for the offer, Sir Alex but I'm afraid the answer has to be 'no'. I'm going to Africa.

Stonor *(His manner changes)* I see. Well, don't come running back here when it all goes pear-shaped. You disappoint me, Standish. I thought you had more about you. Apparently I was wrong. *(Presses intercom on desk)* Felicity, Mr Standish is leaving. And tell Farmer the project meeting is postponed. *(Straightens up and moves towards the window)* We'll have to think of something else, some other time. Goodbye, Standish.

Standish Goodbye, Sir Alex.

He holds out his hand but Stonor has turned his back to gaze out of the window. Standish shrugs his shoulders and exits Left.

Stonor Idiot. *(Remains in position for a few seconds)*

Blackout.

Second Sunday in Lent

Condemnation

In his attack on the Temple traders Jesus was not simply making an OTT intervention in a theological argument; he was condemning the heart of the Jewish nation itself. If these things could be done at the very centre of ecclesiastical and political power, how could God's chosen people be honouring his Father? Since then many Christians have followed his lead in confronting a misuse of power that dishonours God's name. In recent years Martin Luther King, Janani Luwum and Oscar Romero*, among others, have paid for their conviction with their lives. They were condemning racial segregation, corrupt government and the abuse of human rights. Perhaps in this time of Lent, when we think of One who died for what he believed, we should seriously consider the cost of commitment.

Bible source John 2:13-22

Performance time Six minutes with reading

Characters Reader
Anita
Simon
Maria
Carlos
Victor Crespino, a priest

Scene setter *A room, plainly furnished. Downstage Right is a television set with its back to the audience. A small table, two upright chairs and a sofa (two chairs covered with a drape) are ranged in a semicircle from upstage Right to centre Left. A few newspapers, books and cushions complete the picture. Anita is sitting on the sofa reading a newspaper. Victor is off Right ready to speak into a microphone linked to the TV. Simon, Maria and Carlos are off Left. If possible the scene should be in darkness while the Reader, spotlit, is on stage.*

The Reader enters and takes centre stage.

---

* On 24 March 1980 Oscar Romero, Roman Catholic archbishop of San Salvador, who had committed himself to the cause of the poor and the persecuted in the face of a corrupt and violent government, was shot dead while celebrating mass. Some of the phrases used in his sermons and writings are repeated in this sketch.

Reader Jesus clears the Temple.

When it was almost time for the Jewish Passover, Jesus went up to Jerusalem. In the temple courts he found men selling cattle, sheep and doves, and others sitting at tables exchanging money. So he made a whip out of cords, and drove all from the temple area, both sheep and cattle; he scattered the coins of the money-changers and overturned their tables. To those who sold doves he said, 'Get these out of here! How dare you turn my Father's house into a market!'

His disciples remembered that it is written, 'Zeal for your house will consume me.'

Then the Jews demanded of him, 'What miraculous sign can you show us to prove your authority to do all this?'

Jesus answered them, 'Destroy this temple, and I will raise it again in three days.'

The Jews replied, 'It has taken forty-six years to build this temple, and you are going to raise it in three days?' But the temple he had spoken of was his body. After he was raised from the dead, his disciples recalled what he had said. Then they believed the Scripture and the words that Jesus had spoken.

The Reader exits. The scene lights up. Sound of TV turned down – a low background noise of newsreading. Simon enters Left and moves towards Anita.

Simon Has he been on yet?

Anita Not yet. Should be quite soon now. Simon, have you seen this? It's practically a death threat from the Ministry of Justice.

Simon *(Moves to the side of the sofa and bends to read the paper)* 'A catalogue of lies . . . this priest has no place in the church . . . treasonable speeches . . . consequences of further incitement could be fatal . . .' Nothing new there then. It's the mixture as before. Just what we expected.

Anita But 'further incitement could be fatal'. They've never said that before in cold print.

Simon No. That's true enough. But there have been plenty of insinuations on the phone – and in that letter yesterday. *(Grabs a piece of paper from the table)* Where are we? Ah yes '. . . your support of Victor Crespino has been noted and I would strongly advise you and your colleagues not to continue research activities on his behalf. If these activities persist I cannot guarantee your safety.' Cannot guarantee your safety! Ministry of Justice? Ministry of Oppression more like. *(Screws the letter up and throws it across the room)*

Anita Simon, I'm scared.

Simon *(Walks across to Anita and puts a hand on her shoulder)* Come on, chin up. We always knew it might come to this. That time we first heard Victor speak. Do you remember? 'A church that suffers no persecution but enjoys the privileges and support of the things of the earth – beware! – it is not the true Church of Jesus Christ.' That is what we have to hold on to. In all this corruption and betrayal, knowing we are on the side of truth, on the side of Jesus.

Anita Yes, in my heart I know that's right, but in my head I . . .

Maria enters Left. She's out of breath from running and pauses in the doorway to catch her breath. Simon moves quickly to her.

Simon Maria. Are you all right?

Maria Yes, I'm fine. Just give me a minute. I've run all the way from the television studio. *(She holds her side, breathing heavily, and moves to sit with Anita on the sofa)* Ah, that's better.

Anita So what's happening? Did you see Victor? Has he got the new script?

Maria No, I couldn't get through. The foyer was buzzing with ministry officials and there were soldiers at every door turning everyone back. Even the floor manager couldn't get to the transmission room. But I'm sure Victor was inside. That old green Renault he borrows was outside – with a couple of policemen all over it.

Simon That doesn't sound good.

Anita But we were the only ones who knew he was going to broadcast today.

Simon Apart from the guys at the TV station. I don't like the sound of it. First the letter, then this *(he picks up the paper)*, now . . . I think we should pray.

They move together to form a circle, holding hands. Before a word is spoken, Carlos enters Left.

Carlos Well, well, how charming. Where two or three are gathered together in my name . . . or is it just one of those Christian love-ins?

The three loose hands and turn to face Carlos.

Maria What do you mean? Why are you here?

Carlos *(Walks casually across the room)* Oh I just thought you'd like to know that your troublesome priest has had his last warning. Doesn't do to preach the truth to totalitarian governments – as I've mentioned before. No, the Reverend Victor Crespino has spoken out once too often. And if I were you, I would get down to the airport pronto. Not even the consulate can help you now.

Anita *(Points to television)* But he's on! Victor's speaking! *(Brings up the sound with the TV control; Crespino's voice fills the room)*

Crespino . . . A church that suffers no persecution but enjoys the privileges and support of the things of the earth – beware! – is not the true Church of Jesus Christ . . .

Simon Yes, yes.

Crespino A preaching that does not point out sin is not the preaching of the gospel. A preaching that makes sinners feel good, so that they are secured in their sinful state, betrays the gospel's call.

When the Church hears the cry of the oppressed it cannot but denounce the social structures that give rise to and perpetuate the misery from which the cry arises.

The Christian must work to exclude sin and establish God's reign. To struggle for this is not communism . . .

Carlos No, it's idiocy.

Anita Shut up, Carlos. You don't understand.

Crespino To struggle for this is not to mix in politics. It is simply that the gospel demands of today's Christian more commitment to history.

Let us not tire of preaching love, it is the force that will overcome the world. Let us not tire of preaching love. Though we see that waves of violence succeed in drowning the fire of Christian love, love must win out, it is the only thing that can.

A sudden surge of noise – shouting and smashing glass. Then a round of machine-gun fire. Silence. Maria rushes to the TV set and bends to grasp the screen, as if willing the voice and picture to return.

Maria There's nothing. Nothing.

Carlos I told you so. He spoke once too often. *(Moves towards Left and turns back)* Oh, and do remember what I said, won't you? *(Glances at his watch)* They'll be here before long. *(Exits)*

Anita is crying, Maria still looking blankly at the screen, Simon looking after Carlos.

Simon Love must win out. That's what he said. Love must win in the end. Come on you two. It's time to pray.

Slowly the three gather as before; holding hands and bowing their heads. Hold for a moment. Blackout.

Third Sunday in Lent

Confession

The synoptic gospel narratives turn on the one question put by Jesus to his disciples: 'Who do you say that I am?' For two thousand years since that question was put, Christians have echoed Peter's astounding reply: 'The Christ of God.' If that answer is incorrect then all the passion and triumph of Holy Week is a meaningless sham. Yet such is its truth that Peter's confession has sustained and emboldened millions throughout the world who have taken up their cross to follow that same Jesus Christ. One such was Mehdi Dibaj, who was imprisoned for his belief for nine years and in 1994, after a worldwide campaign on his behalf, released, only to be killed shortly afterwards. This monologue is based on his actual final testament, written in prison.

Bible source Luke 9:18-26

Performance time Twelve minutes with reading. If time is a problem paragraphs can be omitted – but take care not to lose the key threads of his argument.

Characters Reader
Mehdi Dibaj – an Iranian pastor, 59

Scene setter *A bare stage. Mehdi Dibaj is writing at a small table. On it is a glass of water, a Bible and two other books. If possible the scene should be in darkness while the Reader, spotlit, is on stage.*

The Reader enters and takes centre stage.

Reader Peter declares the identity of Jesus.

Once when Jesus was praying in private and his disciples were with him, he asked them, 'Who do the crowds say I am?' They replied, 'Some say John the Baptist; others say Elijah; and still others, that one of the prophets of long ago has come back to life.'

'But what about you?' he asked. 'Who do you say I am?' Peter answered, 'The Christ of God.'

Jesus strictly warned them not to tell this to anyone. And he said, 'The Son of Man must suffer many things and be rejected by the elders, chief priests and teachers of the law, and he must be killed and on the third day be raised to life.'

Then he said to them all: 'If anyone would come after me, he must deny himself and take up his cross daily and follow me. For whoever wants to save his life will lose it, but whoever loses his life for me will save it. What good is it for a man to gain the whole world, and yet lose or forfeit his very self? If anyone is ashamed of me and my words, the Son of Man will be ashamed of him when he comes in his glory and in the glory of the Father and of the holy angels.'

Pause.

There was a man in Iran named Mehdi Dibaj, who long ago embraced the Christian religion and had ever since followed his master, Jesus Christ. For this, and only this, he was imprisoned for nine years, was threatened with hanging and only after a worldwide campaign on his behalf was released in January 1994. Six months later he was abducted and murdered. While in prison, awaiting his fate, he wrote his final testament, addressed to his jailers.

Reader exits. Spotlight on Mehdi Dibaj.

Mehdi Dibaj *He finishes writing, sighs, leans back and begins to read the document aloud, declaiming his statement to an imaginary courtroom. Although there is great power in the words themselves, the actor will need to employ a wide variety of tone, gesture and movement to maintain audience attention.*

In the holy name of God who is our life and existence. With all humility I express my gratitude to the Judge of all heaven and earth for this precious opportunity, and with brokenness I wait upon the Lord to deliver me from this court trial according to his promises. I also beg the honoured members of the court who are present to listen with patience to my defence and with respect for the name of the Lord.

I am a Christian. As a sinner I believe Jesus has died for my sins on the cross and by his resurrection and victory over death, has made me righteous in the presence of the holy God. The true God speaks about this fact in his holy word, the gospel. Jesus means Saviour 'because he will save his people from their sins'. Jesus paid the penalty of our sins by his own blood and gave us a new life so that we can live for the glory of God by the help of the Holy Spirit and be like a dam against corruption, be a channel of blessing and healing, and be protected by the love of God.

In response to this kindness, he has asked me to deny myself and be his fully surrendered follower, and not to fear people even if they kill my body, but rather rely on the creator of life who has crowned me with the crown of mercy and compassion. He is the great protector of his beloved ones as well as their great reward.

I have been charged with 'apostasy'! The invisible God who knows our hearts has given assurance to us Christians that we are not among the apostates who will perish but among the believers so that we may save our lives. In Islamic Law an apostate is one who does not believe in God, the prophets or the resurrection of the dead. We Christians believe in all three!

They say 'You were a Muslim and you have become a Christian.' No. For many years I had no religion. After searching and studying I accepted God's call and believed in the Lord Jesus Christ in order to receive eternal life. People choose their religion but a Christian is chosen by Christ. He says, 'You have not chosen me but I have chosen you.' From when? Before the foundation of the world.

People say, 'You were a Muslim from your birth.' God says, 'You were a Christian from the beginning.' He states that he chose us thousands of years ago, even before the creation of the universe, so that through the sacrifice of Jesus Christ we may be his! A Christian means one who belongs to Jesus Christ.

The eternal God who sees the end from the beginning and who has chosen me to belong to him, knew from the beginning those whose heart would be drawn to him and also those who would be willing to sell their faith and eternity for a pot of porridge. I would rather have the whole world against me but know that the almighty God is with me; be called an apostate but know that I have the approval of the God of glory, because man looks at the outward appearance but God looks at the heart. For him who is God for all eternity nothing is impossible. All power in heaven and on earth is in his hands.

The almighty God will raise up anyone he chooses and bring down others, accept some and reject others, send some to heaven and others to hell. Now because God does whatever he desires, who can separate us from the love of God? Or who can destroy the relationship between the creator and the creature or defeat a heart that is faithful to his Lord? He will be safe and secure under the shadow of the Almighty! Our refuge is the mercy seat of God who is exalted from the beginning.

I know in whom I have believed, and he is able to guard what I have entrusted to him to the end, until I reach the kingdom of God, the place where the righteous shine like the sun, but where the evildoers will receive their punishment in hell fire.

They tell me, 'Return!' But to whom can I return from the arms of my God? Is it right to accept what people are saying instead of obeying the word of God? It is now forty-five years that I am walking with the God of miracles, and his kindness upon me is like a shadow and I owe him much for his fatherly love and concern.

The love of Jesus has filled all my being and I feel the warmth of his love in every part of my body. God, who is my glory and honour and protector, has put his seal of approval upon me through his unsparing blessings and miracles.

This test of faith is a clear example. The good and kind God reproves and punishes all those whom he loves. He tests them in preparation for heaven. The God of Daniel, who protected his friends in the fiery furnace, has protected me for nine years in prison. And all the bad happenings have turned out for our good and gain, so much so that I am filled to overflowing with joy and thankfulness.

The God of Job has tested my faith and commitment in order to strengthen my patience and faithfulness. During these nine years he has freed me from all my responsibilities so that under the protection of his blessed name, I would spend my time in prayer and study of his word, with a searching heart and with brokenness, and grow in the knowledge of my Lord. I praise the Lord for this unique opportunity. God gave me space in my confinement, brought healing in my difficult hardships and his kindness revived me. Oh what great blessings God has in store for those who fear him!

They object to my evangelising. But if one finds a blind person who is about to fall into a well and keeps silent then one has sinned. It is our religious duty, as long as the door of God's mercy is open, to convince evildoers to turn from their sinful ways and find refuge in him in order to be saved from the wrath of the righteous God and from the coming dreadful punishment.

Jesus Christ says, 'I am the door. Whoever enters through me will be saved.' 'I am the way, the truth and the life. No one comes to the Father except through me.' 'Salvation is found in no one else, for there is no other name under heaven given to men by which we must be saved.' Among the prophets of God, only Jesus Christ rose from the dead, and he is our living intercessor for ever.

He is our Saviour and he is the Son of God. To know him means to know eternal life. I, a useless sinner, have believed in this beloved person and all his words and miracles recorded in the gospel, and I have committed my life into his hands. Life for me is an opportunity to serve him, and death is a better opportunity to be with Christ. Therefore I am not only satisfied to be in prison for the honour of his holy name, but I am ready to give my life for the sake of Jesus, my Lord, and enter his kingdom sooner, the place where the elect of God enter everlasting life, but the wicked to eternal damnation.

(Stops and considers the paper for a moment) Good. Now just to end. *(Returns to the table, sits down and takes up his pen; he reads the final words as he writes them)*

May the shadow of God's kindness and his hand of blessing and healing be upon you and remain for ever. Amen.

With respect, your Christian prisoner, Mehdi Dibaj.

He continues to sit, staring up in front of him, as, ideally, the lights fade gradually to blackout.

Fourth Sunday in Lent

Recognition

Perhaps in our expectation as we approach the key events of Holy Week we sometimes underestimate the importance of the Transfiguration. It is here that Jesus is revealed as truly divine. It is here that the worlds of the old and new covenants interlock. It is here that not only the chosen three apostles but all of us who call ourselves Christians take a once-in-a-lifetime glance into the radiance of heaven and hear the identity of the Son of God given the unquestionable authority of God the Father. So, this sketch asks, if that identity has been vouched for by the Creator himself then surely we can do nothing less than proclaim it to everyone we know.

Bible source Luke 9:28-36

Performance time Five minutes with reading

Characters Reader
James Talbot, a Christian
Margaret Talbot, his wife
Philip Radcliffe, an agnostic
Susan Radcliffe, his wife

Scene setter *The Talbots' lounge. As much or as little stage dressing as is feasible. Down centre stage is a large rectangular coffee table at which the four actors are sitting; James at the corner back Right with Margaret diagonally opposite him; Philip at the corner back Left with Susan diagonally opposite. They are playing a board game in which one member of a pair describes the word on a card which must be guessed by his or her partner. As many words as possible must be guessed within the thirty seconds designated by a timer (hourglass type). The number of correct answers is then moved forward on a board. There is no need to use an actual board game; miming will be perfectly effective. If possible the scene should be in darkness while the Reader, spotlit, is on stage.*

The Reader enters and takes centre stage.

Reader Jesus is transfigured on the mountain.

Jesus took Peter, John and James with him and went up onto a mountain to pray. As he was praying, the appearance of his face changed, and his clothes became as bright as a flash of lightning. Two men, Moses and Elijah, appeared in glorious splendour, talking with Jesus. They spoke about his departure, which he was about to bring to fulfilment at Jerusalem. Peter and his companions were very sleepy, but when they became fully awake, they saw his glory and the two men standing with him. As the men were leaving Jesus, Peter said to him, 'Master, it is good for us to be here. Let us put up three shelters – one for you, one for Moses and one for Elijah.' (He did not know what he was saying.)

While he was speaking, a cloud appeared and enveloped them, and they were afraid as they entered the cloud. A voice came from the cloud, saying, 'This is my Son, whom I have chosen; listen to him.' When the voice had spoken, they found that Jesus was alone. The disciples kept this to themselves, and told no one at that time what they had seen.

The Reader exits. The scene lights up. Susan is reading a card to Philip. All four are enjoying the game.

Susan Like a toad but lives high up.

Philip Your Uncle Bill. *(The others laugh, including Susan)*

Susan Oh do be serious, Phil. This is a reptile!

Philip Your Uncle Bill! *(Increased laughter)*

James *(Picks up timer)* Time's up you two. What was it Sue?

Susan A tree frog. *(Laughter)* You should have got that Phil.

Philip Ah. Natural history was never my strong point. My form master used to say: 'Radcliffe. Do not contemplate entering the sciences or the church; you have no aptitude for either.'

Margaret Is that why you never go, Phil?

Philip Go where?

Margaret To church. *(Laughingly)* We've asked you enough times.

Susan Oh, he's always got some excuse. Haven't you, darling?

Philip Nothing personal Maggie, but it's really not my cup of tea. *(Hurriedly changing the subject)* Now, what did we score before my gross inability to define a tree frog?

Susan Oh, let's see. *(Counts the cards)* One, two, three, four, five – oh no, we didn't get pineapple, did we – four Margaret.

Margaret *(Moves a counter on the board)* One, two, three, four. Oh, you're ahead now. Come on, James. Show them what you can do.

James Right. *(Takes a pile of cards)* What are we on? Oh, people. OK. Ready when you are.

Philip *(Turns over the timer)* All systems go!

James and Margaret now ad lib in quickly identifying three cards successfully – Margaret Thatcher, Nero and Louis Armstrong.

James *(Putting next card down)* Er – no – pass on that one. *(Looks at next card)* Oh, er . . .

Margaret Come on James, get a move on.

James Er, great teacher, famous preacher . . .

Margaret John Wesley. Martin Luther King. *(James gives negative grunt to both)*

James He – er – healed lots of people.

Margaret Pasteur. Er – Jenner. *(Negative grunts)*

James *(Getting frustrated)* No. Head of a world religion.

Margaret Oh. Buddha. Muhammad.

Philip Time's . . . UP!

James *(Counts cards)* So that's – three. *(Moves counter)* One, two, three. Ah, now *we're* on nature. Better watch out, Phil. Margaret is *very* hot on garden birds. *(Laughter)*

Philip My turn I think. *(Takes cards)*

Margaret *(To James)* So who was it?

James *(Deliberately stalling)* Who was what?

Susan The person you didn't get?

James Oh – er – Jesus Christ.

Philip Now, now Jim. Mind your language. *(The joke falls flat)*

Margaret *(Amazed)* Jesus Christ? *(Puzzled and annoyed)* Why didn't you say who he is?

James *(Buying time; grumpy)* Well, I did. I said he was a great teacher and preacher and head of a world religion. What more do you want?

Margaret You could have said he's the Son of God.

James Well, yes, I suppose so, but I didn't like to . . . well . . .

Margaret You didn't like to say what you believe in front of other people. Is that it?

James *(Riled)* Oh come on. That's not fair. I was simply . . .

Philip *(Enjoying the situation)* Now, now children. Peace and goodwill and all that. *(Playfully to Susan)* Now you see why I don't go to church. Never could grasp this three in one business. *(Picks up cards)* Now, my go I believe. Turn the timer James. What are we?

Susan Er, actions, darling.

Philip Action stations then. *(Looks at first card)* Good heavens. I can't do that.

Susan Oh, what is it?

Philip Transfiguration!

The couples look at each other for a moment before . . .

Blackout.

Fifth Sunday in Lent

Service

As Jesus and the disciples approach Jerusalem, his thoughts are on the unimaginable suffering that lies ahead. Despite yet another clear briefing to the Twelve on the events that will end with his death and their redemption, James and John have thoughts only of preferment in some earthly kingdom over which the Messiah will rule. In response Jesus gives a short lesson on the need for his followers to seek to serve, not to be served. This sketch suggests that the lesson is still relevant.

Bible source Mark 10:32-45

Performance time Seven minutes with reading

Characters Reader
Harry / Harriet – the Vicar / Pastor / Church leader
Ben
Janet
Robert
Sarah
Richard
Monica

Scene setter *A trestle table down centre stage. Harry sits in the centre flanked by Ben and Janet on one side, Robert and Sarah on the other. Richard sits at the short end of the table stage Left. The chair opposite him stage Right is empty, awaiting Monica who is off Right when the action begins. Notepads, papers, pens for each person, a Bible and another book in front of Harry. If possible the scene should be in darkness while the Reader, spotlit, is on stage.*

The Reader enters and takes centre stage.

Reader Jesus reveals his mission.

They were on their way up to Jerusalem, with Jesus leading the way, and the disciples were astonished, while those who followed were afraid. Again he took the Twelve aside and told them what was going to happen to him. 'We are going up to Jerusalem,' he said, 'and the Son of Man will be betrayed to the chief priests and teachers of the law. They will condemn him to death and will hand him over to the Gentiles, who will mock him and spit on him, flog him and kill him. Three days later he will rise.'

Then James and John, the sons of Zebedee, came to him. 'Teacher,' they said, 'we want you to do for us whatever we ask.'

'What do you want me to do for you?' he asked.

They replied, 'Let one of us sit at your right and the other at your left in your glory.'

'You don't know what you are asking,' Jesus said. 'Can you drink the cup I drink or be baptised with the baptism I am baptised with?'

'We can,' they answered.

Jesus said to them, 'You will drink the cup I drink and be baptised with the baptism I am baptised with, but to sit at my right or left is not for me to grant. These places belong to those for whom they have been prepared.'

When the ten heard about this, they became indignant with James and John. Jesus called them together and said, 'You know that those who are regarded as rulers of the Gentiles lord it over them, and their high officials exercise authority over them. Not so with you. Instead, whoever wants to become great among you must be your servant, and whoever wants to be first must be slave of all. For even the Son of Man did not come to be served, but to serve, and to give his life as a ransom for many.'

The Reader exits. The scene lights up. Throughout the sketch Harry addresses the audience as well as the six round the table, as though everybody was attending this church meeting.

Harry *(Looks at watch)* Well, even though Monica's not here yet I think we ought to make a start. *(Glances all round)* Welcome to you all and thank you for coming. I'm sure you agree that it's important to get the new church year off to a sound and sensible start by deciding who is going to take responsibility for our various activities for the next twelve months.

Janet *(Not afraid of putting her point of view)* Hear, hear. Some of last year's arrangements were well below what we should expect.

Harry Perhaps we should be constructive at this meeting rather than critical, Janet.

Janet I speak as I find.

Harry Quite. Quite. *(Consults paper)* Well, first on the list is what I call the Service with a Smile activities. Keeping the place looking cared for. General cleaning, refreshments after services, washing up, the loos . . . not the most glamorous responsibility but absolutely essential. Monica's been doing this for many years now and I'd like her to have a change. What about you, Sarah?

Sarah Well I don't think that's really me, Harry. I'm more the creative type. And I can't really stay after services – too much to do at home.

Harry I see. Ben? You're a practical sort of chap.

Ben Yeees – but not in a washing-up kind of way. *(Laughter from the others)* I see myself as more of an out-front person. Dealing with the press, speaking at meetings – that kind of thing.

Harry Right. What about you, Janet? *(On seeing her expression)* No, on second thoughts, probably not. Well, we'd better leave that one on hold for the moment. *(Turns to paper)* So now it's Public Affairs – press relations, representing the church on various committees, making policy decisions – acting as my right hand in a way.

Ben *(Getting in quickly)* As I've said, I think that's my bag really. I'm pretty well known about the place and I've got some very useful contacts.

Harry *(Not over-enthusiastic)* Well, if you're sure . . .

Ben Absolutely certain, Harry.

Harry Next is, er, Internal Affairs. Organising the prayer meetings, special services, the newsletter, home meetings . . . My left hand ma – person, I should say.

Janet I'd like to nominate Robert. *(Robert grins)*

Harry Really? I was thinking that Monica could . . .

Janet Oh no. Not at all suitable. I think you'll find that Robert will be excellent in the role.

Harry Well, are you willing to take it on, Robert?

Robert *(Grinning)* Oh yes.

Harry *(Sighs)* I see. Well *(consults list)* I presume you'll want to look after the front of house again, Sarah? Flowers, noticeboards, posters, invitations and so on?

Sarah Well, I do believe I have a gift for that kind of artistic expression. And, as Saint Paul says, we must use our gifts, mustn't we? *(She smiles round the table)*

Harry Oh we must. Indeed we must. *(He is not so sure in Sarah's case)*

Richard And I'll be in charge of the technical department again, won't I? After all, I'm the only one who understands the PA system. *(Laughter)*

Harry Yes Richard. Perhaps this year you'll explain how it works to one or two others?

Richard I might. You never know.

Harry So that leaves *(checks list)* Service with a Smile and special events which this year includes the anniversary concert and the televised service. Now . . .

Janet Thank you, Harry. I will take on special events with pleasure.

Harry But I haven't . . .

Janet Of course, it will mean shedding some of my social responsibilities but that is a price I'm willing to pay. In fact *(confidential look all round)* I've already made a tentative suggestion to the television people and they said they were thrilled that I would be working with them.

Harry I see. Well, there doesn't seem much point in discussing it further. So, you all have your responsibilities and that just leaves Monica with . . .

Monica enters out of breath and collapses into her chair.

Monica Oh, I'm so sorry to be late.

Harry I'm sure you had a good reason, Monica.

Monica *(Laughs)* Well, it was just one thing after another. I was mending some of the old hymnbooks when Elsie Cornish rang to ask if I'd run her to the surgery. After that I had to make some cakes for the youth club tomorrow and pop them round to Ian. On the way here I dropped off a newsletter to that couple who've just moved in next to the post office and I would have been here ten minutes ago but some poor child had been sick in the entrance hall and I just had to clean it up.

Harry Monica, there's no need to apologise. You were doing – what you always do. I must apologise to you however because, well, it's still Service with a Smile – if you'll do it.

Monica Of course I'll do it. I'm only too happy to.

Harry Thank you. *(Glances round the table)* And thank you all for coming and for accepting your positions for the coming year with – er – such good grace. *(General nodding and smiling)* My responsibility will of course be Pastoral Care and in light of that I'd like to end this meeting with a quotation from Martin Luther King. *(Opens the book)*

You don't have to have a college degree to serve. You don't have to make your subject and verb agree to serve. You don't have to know Plato and Aristotle. You don't have to know Einstein's theory of relativity. You don't have to know the second theory of thermodynamics in physics. You only need a heart full of grace. A soul generated by love. *(Looks at Monica)*

Pause for a moment.

Blackout.

Palm Sunday

Acclamation

Palm Sunday is the bridge between Lent and Holy Week. Until now the unthinkable reality of the Messiah's arrest, trial and death has been etched only in the mind of Jesus; his followers are still in denial, even though the raising of Lazarus has proved beyond doubt that, when their Master is involved, there is indeed life after death. The decision to go up to Jerusalem for the Passover turns the unthinkable into the probable. Once through the city gate, the lives of this little group of followers spiral inexorably downward into suspicion, betrayal, confusion and flight. The shape of the sketches, too, takes a significant turn. From now on their structure is a series of duologues, using characters – some leading, some supporting – who played a part in the working out of Christ's redeeming mission.

Bible source Matthew 21:1-11

Performance time Five minutes with reading

Characters Reader
Nathan – a merchant
Reuben – a chandler

Scene setter *A street in Bethphage. Nathan is off Right, Reuben off Left.*

The Reader enters and takes centre stage.

Reader Jesus enters Jerusalem.

As they approached Jerusalem and came to Bethphage (Beth-fa-geh) on the Mount of Olives, Jesus sent two disciples, saying to them, 'Go to the village ahead of you, and at once you will find a donkey tied there, with her colt by her. Untie them and bring them to me. If anyone says anything to you, tell him that the Lord needs them, and he will send them right away.'

This took place to fulfil what was spoken through the prophet:

'Say to the Daughter of Zion,
"See, your king comes to you,
gentle and riding on a donkey,
on a colt, the foal of a donkey."'

The disciples went and did as Jesus had instructed them. They brought the donkey and the colt, placed their cloaks on them, and

Jesus sat on them. A very large crowd spread their cloaks on the road, while others cut branches from the trees and spread them on the road. The crowds that went ahead of him and those that followed shouted,

'Hosanna to the Son of David!'
'Blessed is he who comes in the name of the Lord!'
'Hosanna in the highest!'

When Jesus entered Jerusalem, the whole city was stirred and asked, 'Who is this?'

The crowds answered, 'This is Jesus, the prophet from Nazareth in Galilee.'

The Reader exits. Reuben enters Left, slightly before Nathan enters Right.

Reuben Nathan!

Nathan Reuben! *(They embrace)*

Reuben I see the beasts are back.

Nathan The beasts?

Reuben Yes, the donkey and the foal. *(Gestures over his shoulder)*

Nathan Oh, *those* beasts. *(Laughs)* Yes, they're back. One of his followers came over with them this morning. A good deal of thanks but *(he laughs)* no payment! *(Shrugs his shoulders)* Why should I worry? I was happy to loan them. More than happy, seeing it was him. But I'm still puzzled why he did it.

Reuben You saw him start off?

Nathan Yes. I followed them down the Jerusalem road for a while. I was curious to see what he wanted them for. And then they put their cloaks over the animals and he sat on the foal, his feet dangling, almost scraping the ground. At first I laughed out loud. It seemed ridiculous for him to ride that animal into Zion. Some of his followers thought so too; I could see that. But they went along with it; laying their cloaks on the ground in front of him like some royal carpet and throwing down palm fronds. Some shouted 'Hosanna' and a good many other things. As I say, I laughed at first – and so did your wife, she was there along with some other women. But then he turned his head and I saw his face and my laughter died. He was . . . different; older, sterner than I'd seen him before. Looking back up towards the olive trees as though he was seeing them for the last time.

Reuben Yes, he had just that look when he entered the city.

Nathan You saw him in the city?

Reuben Yes, I had to take a batch of candles to the temple. These festivals bring a good trade for some of us. Anyhow, I had a job to get through the crowd. Pilgrims mostly but some Pharisees and the usual hangers-on, all going out of the city to meet him.

Nathan Sightseers no doubt. Heard about that business with Lazarus of Bethany.

Reuben Possibly. Possibly. Whatever the reason, they were making a real din. Singing. Shouting. 'Welcome to David's son' some of them were saying. They seemed to think he's the Messiah.

Nathan Of course! Why didn't I think of that before! It's the Zechariah prophecy, isn't it? Now how does that go? Ah. *(He thinks)* Something about the king will come in peace – riding on an ass! Yes, that's it. Riding on the *foal* of an ass. *That's* why he wanted them.

Reuben Well, whatever the reason, it was as much as I could do to get past into the city. And when the two groups met up – pandemonium!

Nathan I can't believe the Pharisees would have been pleased at that!

Reuben You're not wrong, Nathan, you're not wrong! Long faces! *(They laugh)* And they might have a point. On my way back I heard that he'd been causing trouble in the temple. Attacking the traders apparently, for defiling his father's house. His father's house? It's beyond me.

Nathan But if he *is* the Messiah he'd be attacking the Romans, surely? Not his own people. *(Silence)* No, there's something not right about all this. Did he seem like a conqueror to you? A military leader? *(Reuben shakes his head)* You know, I can't help thinking about when Pilate came down that same road. No donkey for him. A great white horse and half the Roman army clanking along behind. And d'you know, he had that same look. Tight-lipped, stern. But not looking back. No, Reuben. No looking back for that one.

They both turn and look Left for a moment.

Reuben Come on Nathan. Business is good. I'll buy you a drink.

Both exit Right, talking.

Monday in Holy Week

Preparation

The meal in the upper room was in many ways the launch pad for Christ's journey to the cross. It was here he gave his long final briefing to his disciples. It was here he initiated the means by which they were to remember him after he had left them. It was here he showed them the meaning of brotherly love. It was here he prepared them for the arrival of the one who would take his place. It was here he lit the blue touch-paper of betrayal with a look and a word to Judas. For those who were present it was, indeed, a night to remember.

Bible source Luke 22:7-23

Performance time Five minutes with reading

Characters Reader
Peter
John

Scene setter *Peter and John sit on two chairs centre stage, hands clasped, eyes closed in prayer. If possible the scene should be in darkness while the Reader, spotlit, is on stage.*

The Reader enters and takes centre stage.

Reader The Last Supper.

Then came the day of Unleavened Bread on which the Passover lamb had to be sacrificed. Jesus sent Peter and John, saying, 'Go and make preparations for us to eat the Passover.'

'Where do you want us to prepare for it?' they asked.

He replied, 'As you enter the city, a man carrying a jar of water will meet you. Follow him to the house that he enters, and say to the owner of the house, "The Teacher asks: Where is the guest room, where I may eat the Passover with my disciples?" He will show you a large upper room, all furnished. Make preparations there.'

They left and found things just as Jesus had told them. So they prepared the Passover.

When the hour came, Jesus and his apostles reclined at the table. And he said to them, 'I have eagerly desired to eat this Passover with you before I suffer. For I tell you, I will not eat it again until it finds fulfilment in the kingdom of God.'

After taking the cup, he gave thanks and said, 'Take this and divide it among you. For I tell you I will not drink again of the fruit of the vine until the kingdom of God comes.'

And he took bread, gave thanks and broke it, and gave it to them, saying, 'This is my body given for you; do this in remembrance of me.'

In the same way, after the supper he took the cup, saying, 'This cup is the new covenant in my blood, which is poured out for you. But the hand of him who is going to betray me is with mine on the table. The Son of Man will go as it has been decreed, but woe to that man who betrays him.' They began to question among themselves which of them it might be who would do this.

The Reader exits. The scene lights up.

Peter . . . and these things we ask in the name of our dear Lord and Saviour Jesus Christ.

Both Amen. *(They raise their heads)*

Peter They will be ready for us in a moment, brother.

John Yes. And once again we will share the bread and drink the wine as he commanded us to do. *(He touches Peter on the arm)* Do you remember that first time, Peter?

Peter Remember it? It is as clear in my memory as if it were yesterday. It was such a remarkable night. Full of love and fear, brutality and gentleness, teaching and *(his voice breaks)* betrayal.

John But beginning in such a mundane manner. Do you remember his orders? 'Go out and buy what we need.' As if we were a couple of servant girls. *(They laugh)*

Peter Yes. *(Ticks off on his fingers)* Lamb, herbs, bread, wine. It took some time in those crowds of pilgrims to get everything we needed, I remember.

John But at least we didn't have to worry about finding a room.

Peter No. He'd planned for that – as he planned for everything in that week. And do you remember the man with the water pot? That was a stroke of genius. Whoever heard of a man carrying water! *(They laugh)*

John *(Deep in thought)* What a meal that was. Has there ever been anything quite like it? Not the food, of course. We all knew that from childhood. But what it led to.

Peter Yes. So much from a single word. 'Go, do what you have to do.' I can see Iscariot's face now, in the lamplight; a kind of painful resignation to what he had agreed.

John And what did we do? Nothing. Yes, it seemed a little odd at the time but he was always out and about on some charitable business or other. If only we'd known.

Peter And what if we had? Could we have stopped what was to come? No. The master had planned out his death just as he'd planned the supper. And thank God he did. Otherwise we would not be remembering his sacrifice now in bread and wine. Otherwise we would not be filled with the Holy Spirit as he promised. Otherwise we would not be expecting his return from God the Father to whom we saw him leave.

John No, you're right, brother. Of course you're right. He knew exactly what he was doing. *(In thought)* 'This is my body given for you; do this in remembrance of me.' I can still see the expression on his face as he broke the bread.

Peter And then at the end of the meal he took the cup. *(He raises his hands)* 'This cup is the new covenant in my blood, which is poured out for you.'

John There will be some here tonight who will not have heard that story.

Peter There will indeed, brother. And we shall tell it and tell it again and perhaps commit it to writing, until he comes again as he promised.

John Amen to that, brother. *(Rises)* They will be ready for us now.

Peter They will. *(He rises)* Lead on, John. I will follow. Remember what he said? The first shall be last and the last first.

Laughing quietly they exit Right.

Tuesday in Holy Week

Betrayal

The betrayal of Jesus in the Passion story takes many forms. Our eyes naturally fix on Judas Iscariot, whose part in the sequence of events still arouses theological controversy. But what of Peter, soon to become the head of the fledging Church? What of the rest of the apostles, scattered like chaff? What of the crowd with their shouts of 'Crucify'? What of the self-interested chief priests and the politically-motivated Roman governor? Each in their turn rejects the Son of Man and in this sketch it is, as always, the disinterested onlookers who see most of the game.

Bible source Luke 22:39-62

Performance time Six minutes with reading

Characters Reader
Malchus – servant of the High Priest
Ruth – another servant

Scene setter *Malchus sits right of centre stage, reading from a scroll across his knees. In front of him is a charcoal brazier with its light off. Ruth is off Left with an earthenware mug. If possible the scene should be in darkness while the Reader, spotlit, is on stage.*

The Reader enters and takes centre stage.

Reader Jesus prays on the Mount of Olives, is arrested and disowned by Peter.

Jesus went out as usual to the Mount of Olives, and his disciples followed him. On reaching the place, he said to them, 'Pray that you will not fall into temptation.' He withdrew about a stone's throw beyond them, knelt down and prayed, 'Father, if you are willing, take this cup from me; yet not my will, but yours be done.' An angel from heaven appeared to him and strengthened him. And being in anguish, he prayed more earnestly, and his sweat was like drops of blood falling to the ground.

When he rose from prayer and went back to the disciples, he found them asleep, exhausted from sorrow. 'Why are you sleeping?' he asked them. 'Get up and pray so that you will not fall into temptation.'

While he was still speaking a crowd came up, and the man who was called Judas, one of the Twelve, was leading them. He approached Jesus to kiss him, but Jesus asked him, 'Judas, are you betraying the Son of Man with a kiss?'

When Jesus' followers saw what was going to happen, they said, 'Lord, should we strike with our swords?' And one of them struck the servant of the high priest, cutting off his right ear.

But Jesus answered, 'No more of this!' And he touched the man's ear and healed him.

Then Jesus said to the chief priests, the officers of the temple guard, and the elders, who had come for him, 'Am I leading a rebellion, that you have come with swords and clubs? Every day I was with you in the temple courts, and you did not lay a hand on me. But this is your hour—when darkness reigns.'

Then seizing him, they led him away and took him into the house of the high priest. Peter followed at a distance. But when they had kindled a fire in the middle of the courtyard and had sat down together, Peter sat down with them. A servant girl saw him seated there in the firelight. She looked closely at him and said, 'This man was with him.'

But he denied it. 'Woman, I don't know him,' he said.

A little later someone else saw him and said, 'You also are one of them.'

'Man, I am not!' Peter replied.

About an hour later another asserted, 'Certainly this fellow was with him, for he is a Galilean.'

Peter replied, 'Man, I don't know what you're talking about!' Just as he was speaking, the rooster crowed. The Lord turned and looked straight at Peter. Then Peter remembered the word the Lord had spoken to him: 'Before the rooster crows today, you will disown me three times.' And he went outside and wept bitterly.

The Reader exits. The scene and the brazier light up. Malchus warms his hands as Ruth enters and goes towards him.

Ruth Here, Malchus. Get this down you. It's a cold night for sitting around. *(Pulls her coat round her)*

Malchus *(Scrambling to his feet and taking the mug)* Thanks, Ruth. That's very good of you. *(Takes a mouthful)* Um. Just the job. I needed to get some air. What's going on inside?

Ruth Oh, the guards are having their usual fun. Aaron is there and you know what he's like. 'Let the poor man alone', I said to them. 'What harm has he done you?' But they just laughed.

Malchus He's a good man, Ruth. I'm sure of that. You heard about my ear? *(He touches it)*

Ruth Yes, Esther in the kitchen was telling me. I couldn't believe it. It was really cut off?

Malchus It really was. One of his followers had a sword and just as the guards made the arrest he made a sort of lunge forward and caught the side of my head. *(Puts up his hand again)* It was such a shock; the flesh all torn away and the blood running through my fingers. I felt faint and just dropped to my knees.

Ruth O-er. Makes me feel faint just to hear about it. Then what happened?

Malchus Well, this man Jesus just put his hand over my ear and when he took it away *(he takes his hand away)* the wound was healed. It was as though nothing had happened. And then he told his people to put their weapons away. 'This is not the way', he said. *(He pauses to drink)* You know, when he touched me it was like sometimes when I'm polishing those bronze vases in the house when the air's dry. A shock of power. And standing there in the torchlight he seemed for a moment – kind of invincible, as if nothing could touch him. All the crowd felt it I think, even the guards. But then the moment passed and he let them bind him and rough him up and take him away, as quiet as a lamb.

Ruth I feel sorry for him, I really do. Seems as if everyone's taken against him, even those who were close to him. That chap Iscariot for one.

Malchus Oh, Judas. I was with him at the arrest. Tried to talk to him about what this Jesus of Nazareth was really up to but he didn't say much. Seemed quite bitter about the whole business.

Ruth He came back here you know. He was in a bad way. Shouting and swearing and trying to give the money back. But they weren't interested. Pushed him out. Well, they'd got what they wanted, hadn't they?

Malchus And the others just vanished into the night. Not that we had any orders to arrest them. It was Jesus they wanted.

Ruth One of them was here not half an hour ago. Skulking around. Big man. I could tell he was a Northerner as soon as he opened his mouth. 'You with this Jesus of Nazareth, then?' I said. 'No', he said, 'I don't know who you're talking about.' Well, that was a lie because one of the guards recognised him from when they made the arrest. Anyway, he went on denying it, quite aggressive he was. Then suddenly he sort of crumpled up, broke down, started crying. 'What's up with you?' I said. But he just turned round and went away.

Malchus Well, it must have been a shock for all of them. Only the other day he was being given the VIP treatment. Some people *(hand over his mouth and whispering)* including one or two not far from here, *(normal voice)* thought he might be the Messiah.

Ruth Well, whoever he thinks he is, he's for it and no mistake. They're planning a full meeting of the Sanhedrin tonight so that they can get him tried and into Pilate for sentencing before the Sabbath.

Malchus But that's illegal, isn't it?

Ruth Huh. You try telling that to Caiaphas. No, it's curtains for the preacher Malchus, you mark my words. Brr, it's cold out here. You finished that wine? *(Malchus takes a final gulp and gives her the mug)* Time to go back inside. I've still got work to do and you'll be needed before the night's out. *(She begins to walk off Left)*

Malchus Yes, I'm coming. Perhaps I'll be able to see him again. *(Follows her off)* I didn't really have the chance to say thank you.

Wednesday in Holy Week

Examination

To put the Son of God on trial seems the gravest blasphemy. To attempt to judge the one who had healed the sick, restored the lost, challenged the worldly, forgiven the sinner, raised the dead. To judge a man for the one action he could not avoid; admitting who he was. The powers of this world – both secular and religious – connive at his sentence; Pilate and Caiaphas alike fearing for their own prestige. In the heat of the moment the crowd exercise mob justice and the soldiery simply obey orders. As in many later trial stories a message is delivered at the last minute but this time there is no happy reprieve.

Bible source Matthew 27:1-2, 11-26

Performance time Five minutes with reading

Characters Reader
Claudia – Pilate's wife
Sabina (servant)
Marius (servant)

Scene setter *Claudia's dressing room. Chairs, a table, and a large mirror in which she is checking her make-up. Some combs and a brush on the table. Sabina and Marius are off Left. If possible the scene should be in darkness while the Reader, spotlit, is on stage.*

The Reader enters and takes centre stage.

Reader Jesus before Pilate.

Early in the morning, all the chief priests and the elders of the people came to the decision to put Jesus to death. They bound him, led him away and handed him over to Pilate, the governor.

Meanwhile Jesus stood before the governor, and the governor asked him, 'Are you the king of the Jews?'

'Yes, it is as you say,' Jesus replied.

When he was accused by the chief priests and the elders, he gave no answer. Then Pilate asked him, 'Don't you hear the testimony they are bringing against you?' But Jesus made no reply, not even to a single charge – to the great amazement of the governor.

Now it was the governor's custom at the Feast to release a prisoner chosen by the crowd. At that time they had a notorious prisoner, called Barabbas. So when the crowd had gathered, Pilate asked them, 'Which one do you want me to release to you: Barabbas, or Jesus who is called Christ?' For he knew it was out of envy that they had handed Jesus over to him.

While Pilate was sitting on the judge's seat, his wife sent him this message: 'Don't have anything to do with that innocent man, for I have suffered a great deal today in a dream because of him.'

But the chief priests and the elders persuaded the crowd to ask for Barabbas and to have Jesus executed.

'Which of the two do you want me to release to you?' asked the governor. 'Barabbas,' they answered.

'What shall I do, then, with Jesus who is called Christ?' Pilate asked.

They all answered, 'Crucify him!'

'Why? What crime has he committed?' asked Pilate.

But they shouted all the louder, 'Crucify him!'

When Pilate saw that he was getting nowhere, but that instead an uproar was starting, he took water and washed his hands in front of the crowd. 'I am innocent of this man's blood,' he said. 'It is your responsibility!'

All the people answered, 'Let his blood be on us and on our children!'

Then he released Barabbas to them. But he had Jesus flogged, and handed him over to be crucified.

The Reader exits. The scene lights up. Looking in the mirror, Claudia pats her hair, moves anxiously to back Left and leans out, looking over an imaginary balcony and, distracted, goes back to the mirror again. Sabina runs in from Left.

Claudia *(Moving towards her)* At last! Did you give him the message?

Sabina Yes, my lady. But he had already spoken to the prisoner. I had to go out to the judgement seat. You should have seen the crowd. Thousands, tens of thousands.

Claudia And what did my lord Pilate say?

Sabina He spoke to the people and the Jewish leaders. He said that in honour of their festival he was willing to release a prisoner to them.

Claudia *(Excited)* This man Jesus?

Sabina Well, yes, Jesus *or* someone called Barabbas.

Claudia Barabbas? I seem to have heard that name. *(A moment's thought)* No, I can't remember. So what happened?

Sabina There was a lot of discussion among the crowd. The priests were going round talking to the people. Then I came away. Marius stayed. He'll come back when it's all over.

Claudia And my lord Pilate. How did he seem?

Sabina Oh, he was in good voice my lady. But . . . *(she pauses)*

Claudia But what girl? Speak up. We have no secrets, have we?

Sabina He seemed a little – out of sorts, my lady. Irritated – by the noise and those Jewish leaders I would think. And he kept *(pauses)* turning to look at the prisoner. As I was leaving he called for wine.

Claudia *(Starts pacing the room)* He must release him! He must! That dream was so vivid. This man Jesus of Nazareth was there, his face creased in agony, and my lord Pilate was looking on. He was washing his hands in a bowl and when he took them out they were covered in – blood. *(She breaks off and grips the back of a chair)* And then everything went black and I heard a loud voice – you are killing God. You are killing God. It was dreadful.

Sabina *(Goes to her as if to comfort her)* I know, my lady. I heard you cry out.

Claudia But what if this man is a god of some kind and they kill him. I could never forgive myself. *(Distraught)*

Sabina Come, my lady, sit down. Let me brush your hair for a while. You must be calm. *(Takes a hairbrush from the table)*

Claudia Yes, yes, Sabina. *(Sits down)* You're right. I must be calm. It would never do for your master to see me like this. *(Turns to look at Sabina)* Thank you. You're a good girl. *(Sabina brushes Claudia's hair)* Listen! What was that?

Sabina What, my lady?

Claudia I thought I heard something. Shouting. *(Goes over to balcony again and turns towards Left)* No, nothing. The streets are deserted.

Sabina *(Goes to her)* Come and sit down again, my lady. Marius will be back soon. You can't do any more.

Claudia No. You're right. I have done all I can.

As they move back across the stage Marius enters Left, out of breath.

Marius My lady! It's all over!

Claudia *(Rushes across to Marius and grasps his arms)* What do you mean, it's all over?

Marius When my lord Pilate offered the people the choice between Barabbas and Jesus, they chose – Barabbas.

Claudia *(Slowly)* They chose – Barabbas. Then what of the man Jesus? What of him?

Marius *(Slowly)* He is to be crucified, my lady.

Claudia takes a sharp intake of breath, lets go of Marius and walks slowly to a chair, centre. She sits and looks down Right at the floor. A pause. She turns back to Marius.

Claudia And what of my lord Pilate?

Marius He would have nothing to do with it. He sent for a bowl of water and washed his hands.

Sabina *(Puts her hand to her mouth)* The dream! Your dream, my lady! He washed his hands . . .

Claudia . . . in blood. Yes, Sabina, he washed his hands in the blood . . . of a god. *(She turns her head from one to the other as she speaks)* What has he done? What have we all done?

Blackout.

Maundy Thursday

Humility

It seems entirely appropriate that on the day before we remember the death of Jesus, we commemorate his command (in French *mandé*) to his disciples to wash each other's feet, following his example. This washing, as they sat in the upper room beginning the Passover meal, was one of those extraordinary moments in Jesus' ministry when he completely overturned accepted custom; dining with tax collectors, talking to a Samaritan woman, touching lepers. Although this foot washing is still repeated in some parts of the Christian world as a symbolic act, we need to find a deeper level of understanding in the picture of the Son of God with a towel round his waist, bending over the dirty feet of his followers. It was a picture he intended them to fix in their minds to motivate their behaviour long after he had died, risen and ascended. The Last Supper was a remarkable meal and it would seem quite feasible that when it was over the two disciples who had prepared it would be the last to leave.

Bible source John 13:1-15

Performance time Five minutes with reading

Characters Reader
Peter
John

Scene setter *The playing area is in darkness while the Reader, spotlit, is on stage. Peter and John are both off Right.*

The Reader enters and takes centre stage.

Reader Jesus washes his disciples' feet.

It was just before the Passover Feast. Jesus knew that the time had come for him to leave this world and go to the Father. Having loved his own who were in the world, he now showed them the full extent of his love.

The evening meal was being served, and the devil had already prompted Judas Iscariot, son of Simon, to betray Jesus. Jesus knew that the Father had put all things under his power, and that he had come from God and was returning to God; so he got up from the meal, took off his outer clothing, and wrapped a towel round his waist. After that, he poured water into a basin and began to wash his disciples' feet, drying them with the towel that was wrapped round him.

He came to Simon Peter, who said to him, 'Lord, are you going to wash my feet?'

Jesus replied, 'You do not realise now what I am doing, but later you will understand.'

'No,' said Peter, 'you shall never wash my feet.' Jesus answered, 'Unless I wash you, you have no part with me.'

'Then, Lord,' Simon Peter replied, 'not just my feet but my hands and my head as well!'

Jesus answered, 'A person who has had a bath needs only to wash his feet; his whole body is clean. And you are clean, though not every one of you.' For he knew who was going to betray him, and that was why he said not every one was clean.

When he had finished washing their feet, he put on his clothes and returned to his place. 'Do you understand what I have done for you?' he asked them. 'You call me "Teacher" and "Lord", and rightly so, for that is what I am. Now that I, your Lord and Teacher, have washed your feet, you also should wash one another's feet. I have set you an example that you should do as I have done for you.'

The Reader exits. The scene lights up. Peter walks on from Right, looking back and waving a hand. John follows him.

Peter Goodnight.

John Goodnight – and thank you again.

Peter What an evening! I tell you John, my head is spinning!

John Yes, mine too! So much to take in.

They pause centre stage.

Peter The things he said. The bread – his body, the wine – his blood. I couldn't get my head round that. And all that about his going away and sending someone else to take his place. And saying one of us would betray him. Us, who would go to hell and back for him!

John And what about when he washed our feet, Peter? Extraordinary!

Peter A servant's job. Nothing but a servant's job. That's why I told him he wasn't to wash *my* feet.

John But he did. He washed the feet of every one of us. *(Ticks off the names on his fingers)* Me, you, James, Andrew, Matthew, Philip, James, Thomas, Bartholomew, Simon, Judas and Judas Iscariot.

Peter *(A thought strikes him)* And do you know what? Not one of us offered to wash *his* feet. I should have thought of that.

John No, Peter. I don't think he would have wanted that. Do you remember what he said? Something like, 'This is an example for you. Just as I have washed *your* feet so you should wash one another's.'

Peter *(Puzzled)* But that would be a bit complicated, wouldn't it? All of us going round washing each other's feet?

John No, I don't think he meant we should *actually* wash each other's feet. It's more like one his parables. It has another meaning. He wants us to defer to each other, serve each other, show the humility to others that he showed to us this evening. *(Pause; he looks up at the sky)* Time's getting on. We'd better hurry after the others.

Peter *(Catches his arm)* Wait just a moment, John. You're the closest to him of all of us. What's going to happen now? What has he said?

John I wish I knew. After those shouts of Hallelujah when he entered the city I thought he would – reveal himself somehow as the chosen one, Messiah. But all this talk of suffering and death – and going away. Is that really going to happen? Or does he mean something else by it?

Peter How can we tell? Remember how furious he was when I suggested such things were not to happen to him?

John Yes. It's as though his future is planned out for him and he won't turn aside from it, no matter what happens.

Peter It's a strange business and no mistake. Here am I, a Galilee fisherman, walking round Jerusalem in the middle of the night, with an old sword *(he slaps his left side with his right hand)* like some mountain bandit and knowing nothing of what's to come. *(Slight pause)* Except that Jesus of Nazareth *is* the Christ, the Son of the living God. And that I intend to stick with him through thick and thin.

John And so do we all, Peter. Although – I have my doubts about Iscariot.

Peter Yes, why did he go off that like that, in the middle of the meal?

John I don't know, but there was something – not quite right about it. I was lying next to Jesus as you know and when he passed Judas the soaked bread it was as though he was committing himself to something from which there was no going back. And when he told him to go –'do what you have to do', I think he said – there was such a strange look in Judas' eyes; almost of fear, but fear mixed with shame. But whether that was to do with the master or himself or was about something entirely different, I couldn't say.

Peter Well they were both acting strangely, if you ask me. Perhaps we'll find out more when we see them again. Well, we'd better be going. They'll be at the garden by now. At least we'll be able to have a good rest when we get there. *(Begins to move off Left)*

John *(Following him)* Yes, that's something to look forward to. Mind what you're doing with that sword. You could give someone a nasty injury.

They laugh as they exit.

Good Friday

Crucifixion

As the great drama of Holy Week nears its close, Jesus takes up his cross and is lifted up as he had predicted. Around it gathers a representative selection of humanity whose counterparts are with us today: close at hand the true believers and the critics, further away the disinterested passers-by and, somewhere in between, those – like Simon the sign-writer – who just can't make up their mind about Jesus of Nazareth, King of the Jews.

Bible source John 19:16-30

Performance time Six minutes with reading

Characters Reader
Simon – a sign-writer
Baruch – a trader

Scene setter *Simon stands Right of centre, looking out over the audience. Baruch is off Left. If possible the scene should be in darkness while the Reader, spotlit, is on stage.*

The Reader enters and takes centre stage.

Reader The Crucifixion.

Finally Pilate handed him over to them to be crucified.

So the soldiers took charge of Jesus. Carrying his own cross, he went out to the place of the Skull (which in Aramaic is called Golgotha). Here they crucified him, and with him two others – one on each side and Jesus in the middle.

Pilate had a notice prepared and fastened to the cross. It read: JESUS OF NAZARETH, THE KING OF THE JEWS. Many of the Jews read this sign, for the place where Jesus was crucified was near the city, and the sign was written in Aramaic, Latin and Greek. The chief priests of the Jews protested to Pilate, 'Do not write "The King of the Jews", but that this man claimed to be king of the Jews.'

Pilate answered, 'What I have written, I have written.'

When the soldiers crucified Jesus, they took his clothes, dividing them into four shares, one for each of them, with the undergarment remaining. This garment was seamless, woven in one piece from top to bottom.

'Let's not tear it,' they said to one another. 'Let's decide by lot who will get it.'

This happened that the Scripture might be fulfilled which said, 'They divided my garments among them and cast lots for my clothing.' So this is what the soldiers did.

Near the cross of Jesus stood his mother, his mother's sister, Mary the wife of Clopas, and Mary Magdalene. When Jesus saw his mother there, and the disciple whom he loved standing near by, he said to his mother, 'Dear woman, here is your son,' and to the disciple, 'Here is your mother.' From that time on, this disciple took her into his home.

Later, knowing that all was now completed, and so that the Scripture would be fulfilled, Jesus said, 'I am thirsty.' A jar of wine vinegar was there, so they soaked a sponge in it, put the sponge on a stalk of the hyssop plant, and lifted it to Jesus' lips. When he had received the drink, Jesus said, 'It is finished.' With that, he bowed his head and gave up his spirit.

The Reader exits. The scene lights up. Baruch enters carrying a bag over his shoulder. He is about to pass upstage but notices Simon and comes over to stand beside him, putting his bag on the ground.

Baruch Another execution! One would think the Romans had enough blood on their hands already.

Simon *(Turns to him, speaking softly)* It is not wise to criticise the Romans, friend. Particularly at this time when revolt is in the air.

Baruch Oh, revolt is always in the air somewhere in the great empire. Here, in my own country, even in Rome itself, I hear. But nothing ever comes of it. People are fatalistic. If it were not Rome it would be another great power. The devil you know . . . *(He laughs)* Besides, they bring civilisation of a sort – plumbing and circuses. *(They both laugh)*

Simon What is your business, friend?

Baruch Oh, spices, perfumes, nard. *(He taps the bag)* Always in demand at these festivals. I follow the crowds from one city to another. And you?

Simon A sign-writer. You can see an example of my work up there. *(Points)* Above that cross in the centre of the three.

Baruch *(Peering up)* I commend your skill, my friend. Finely written. I can read the Greek and Latin – but not the . . .

Simon Aramaic.

Baruch Ah yes. Aramaic. What does it say? The King of the Jews. King of the Jews? Surely they are not crucifying your king?

Simon To tell you the truth, I don't know who they're crucifying. The man, Jesus of Nazareth he is called, was a teacher and healer.

There are many such as he in our country. For the past three years he has been travelling around with a small group of followers. The common people loved him; called him a prophet, perhaps Elijah come back to us. Some even believed he was Messiah.

Baruch Messiah? Is that a king?

Simon Of a kind, yes. Our holy scriptures promise that one day Messiah will come and put all things right. He is to be of the house of David and he will rule over his people for ever, from this city of Jerusalem, the holy city.

Baruch *(Points)* Listen, your king cries out. He is thirsty. Ah, they are putting some wine on a sponge and raising it to his lips. *(Pause)* He drinks.

Simon It will be wretched stuff. Not fit for a king.

Baruch But fit for a criminal. For only criminals are crucified by the Romans, are they not? Criminals and slaves.

Simon Pilate could find no crime against him. He wanted to let him go. But the scribes and the Pharisees had it in for him. They've been against him from the start, ever since he said he could forgive sins.

Baruch Forgive sins! But in your religion – forgive me if I am wrong – sins can only be forgiven by God.

Simon Exactly. So he was saying, in what he did and what he said, that he *was* Messiah, in the Greek Christos, he who should come. And they wouldn't have that. Nor, in the end, would the people. And nor, so I've heard, would his followers. Everyone has denied or deserted him.

Baruch And what about Rome?

Simon Oh, as I say, Pilate would have let him go but in the end the religious lobby had its way. He couldn't afford to offend them again. But that sign of mine is his way of getting his own back. Jesus of Nazareth, the king of the Jews. You should have seen the look on those high priestly faces when the soldiers tacked that up! Stuck in their craw it did.

Baruch He speaks again. I can't quite hear. His head drops. The women there cry out. It is the end for your king, my friend.

Simon Yes, I suppose it is. It's funny, you know, I never thought it would come to this. Even when he was being lashed. Even when he was on the cross. I half expected him to come into his own. To come down from the cross and prove his enemies wrong.

Baruch *(Puts a hand on Simon's shoulder)* No, my friend. The only way your king will come down from that cross is for burial. Who knows, he might even be a good customer for me. *(Pats his bag)* Speaking of which I must be going. *(Looking up)* It's getting quite dark. Goodbye, my friend. May your God be with you.

Simon Goodbye. May you prosper. *(Turns back to look for the last time)* Jesus of Nazareth, The King of the Jews. Fair writing under pressure, though I say it myself. But who were you? Preacher? Teacher? Healer? False prophet? Not Messiah at any rate. No son of God would finish up dead on a Roman cross. *(Turns to walk off Right)* That's only for criminals – and slaves. *(Exits)*

Blackout.

Easter Day

Resurrection

The first Easter Day was a time for communication. The message was starkly simple – Jesus of Nazareth was alive! It passed like wildfire between his disciples and was received with varying degrees of incredulity, disbelief and joy. Last of all on that first day of a new era it was communicated by the risen Christ himself to a couple of ordinary followers in their own home. Their response is an encouragement to all of us who have received the Good News.

Bible source Luke 24:13-35

Performance time Six minutes with reading

Characters Reader
Cleopas
Benjamin

Scene setter *A table and three chairs. On the table a bowl of fruit, plates and glasses, a wine bottle, a lamp and a Bible. Perhaps a broom in one corner and somewhere to hang clothes. Back Right another table or cupboard to act as a sink. Some glasses and mugs on top of it. Cleopas and Benjamin are off Left. If possible the scene should be in darkness while the Reader, spotlit, is on stage.*

The Reader enters and takes centre stage.

Reader On the road to Emmaus.

Now that same day two of them were going to a village called Emmaus, about seven miles from Jerusalem. They were talking with each other about everything that had happened. As they talked and discussed these things with each other, Jesus himself came up and walked along with them; but they were kept from recognising him.

He asked them, 'What are you discussing together as you walk along?'

They stood still, their faces downcast. One of them, named Cleopas, asked him, 'Are you only a visitor to Jerusalem and do not know the things that have happened there in these days?'

'What things?' he asked.

'About Jesus of Nazareth,' they replied. 'He was a prophet, powerful in word and deed before God and all the people. The chief priests and our rulers handed him over to be sentenced to death, and they crucified him; but we had hoped that he was the one who was going to redeem Israel. And what is more, it is the third day since all this took place. In addition, some of our women amazed us. They went to the tomb early this morning but didn't find his body. They came and told us that they had seen a vision of angels, who said he was alive. Then some of our companions went to the tomb and found it just as the women had said, but him they did not see.'

He said to them, 'How foolish you are, and how slow of heart to believe all that the prophets have spoken! Did not the Christ have to suffer these things and then enter his glory?' And beginning with Moses and all the Prophets, he explained to them what was said in all the Scriptures concerning himself.

As they approached the village to which they were going, Jesus acted as if he were going farther. But they urged him strongly, 'Stay with us, for it is nearly evening; the day is almost over.' So he went in to stay with them.

When he was at the table with them, he took bread, gave thanks, broke it and began to give it to them. Then their eyes were opened and they recognised him, and he disappeared from their sight. They asked each other, 'Were not our hearts burning within us while he talked with us on the road and opened the Scriptures to us?'

They got up and returned at once to Jerusalem. There they found the Eleven and those with them, assembled together and saying, 'It is true! The Lord has risen and has appeared to Simon.' Then the two told what had happened on the way, and how Jesus was recognised by them when he broke the bread.

The Reader exits. The scene lights up. Cleopas and Benjamin enter from Left, both cheerful. They are wearing coats or raincoats.

Cleopas *(Taking off his coat and hanging it up)* Home again! I can't believe we've been there and back again. *(Goes across to the table and switches on the lamp)*

Benjamin *(Taking off his coat and hanging it up)* No. I should feel tired out but I'm still bubbling with excitement. He's alive! *(Comes to face Cleopas)* He's actually alive!

Cleopas I know. It's . . . Incredible! Miraculous! Fantastic! But alive or not, these things won't wash themselves. *(Starts clearing the table to the sink)*

Benjamin *(Goes to help)* Now that *would* be a miracle. *(Holds up wine bottle)* There's still half a bottle here. Fancy a glass?

Cleopas Yes, all right. I'll just get some clean glasses. *(Brings two glasses from the back table and sits down while Benjamin pours the wine)*

Benjamin Just imagine. It was only a few hours ago since he was sitting on that very same chair. Jesus Christ! The one we had all given up on. The one who was crucified, dead and buried.

Cleopas I know. It's just so difficult to take in. But how could we have been so blind! I mean, it was all there, in the scriptures, *(picks up the Bible)* just like he said.

Benjamin You foolish people! So slow to believe the message of the prophets. I thought you were going to burst a blood vessel when he said that.

Cleopas Well I didn't know who he was, did I? Thought he was just some religious know-all. But then, when he began to speak, well, it all seemed as clear as crystal. It was just as he said; he had to suffer and die before he could enter into his glory.

Benjamin And when he was talking we both felt that kind of inner glow that we always felt when we were the Lord, didn't we?

Cleopas We certainly did. I knew at the time there was something special about him, but I couldn't put my finger on it, not even when he was sitting at this table. Not until he broke the bread.

Benjamin *(Standing up)* How many people, Cleopas? How many people have entertained the Son of God to supper?

Cleopas Well, quite a number over these last three years. But no one else has entertained the *resurrected* Son of God to supper – that's the difference.

Benjamin But what difference will it make, his resurrection? Will things go back to how they were before?

Cleopas We can't fully know yet. It's all so new, so incredible. But now that he's beaten death, well, nothing is impossible! What did we see in the faces of the others in Jerusalem? John and Peter and Matthew and the Marys?

Not just relief and joy and amazement but hope. Hope for the future. A future in which he'll be with us for ever.

Benjamin Steady on. You'll be turning into a preacher in a minute!

Cleopas Well, something radical has happened today, hasn't it? Our world's been stood on its head. Our lord and master Jesus Christ was dead and is alive again. And we have to shout that from the housetops.

Benjamin *We* have to? Surely that's for the big men in Jerusalem – the twelve.

Cleopas Eleven now.

Benjamin All right, eleven. But it'll still be them doing the talking; James and John and Peter.

Cleopas Don't you believe it. This is good news and we've got to spread it. *(Picks up the Bible, goes to coats, takes his down and starts to put it on)* Come on.

Benjamin Come on where?

Cleopas Door-to-door visiting.

Benjamin *(Looks at his watch)* But it's two in the morning.

Cleopas All the more reason. Everyone will be in. Come on!

Benjamin All right. *(Gets coat and follows Cleopas out of the door Left, laughing)* You foolish person!

Blackout.